NIGHT AT THE MUSEUM 2™
ACTIVITY BOOK

First published in the UK by
HarperCollins Children's Books in 2009

1 3 5 7 9 10 8 6 4 2
ISBN-13: 978-0-00-784732-7

Night at the Museum 2™ and © 2009 Twentieth Century Fox Film Corporation.
All rights reserved.

Printed and bound in UK

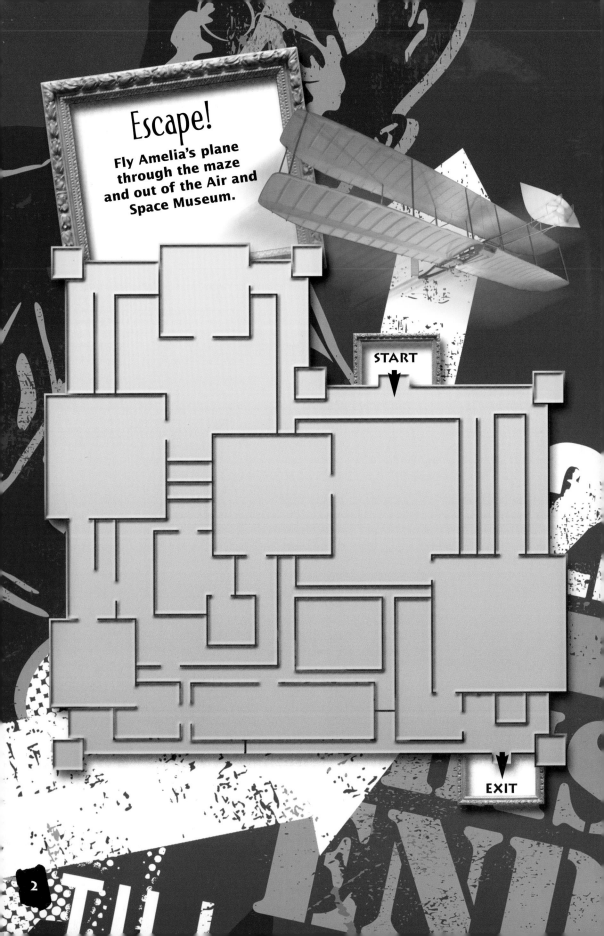

Escape!

Fly Amelia's plane through the maze and out of the Air and Space Museum.

START

EXIT

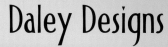
Daley Designs

Larry Daley is famous for his inventions that make life easier. If you could invent something to help you out, what would it be? Design your device below.

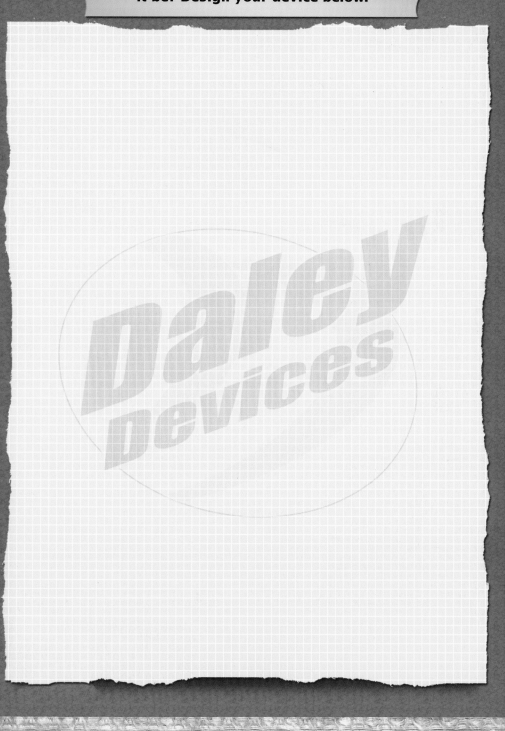

Good Guys Wordsearch

See if you can find all the good guys in this wordsearch. They can be hidden horizontally, vertically, diagonally and even backwards!

Able
Abraham Lincoln
Dexter

General Custer
Amelia Earhart

Larry Daley
Octavius
Jedediah

Sacajawea
Theodore Roosevelt

T	Q	R	Y	U	I	O	L	J	G	F	S	A	Z	C	B	M
O	H	G	J	K	Y	T	R	E	W	B	D	G	H	B	V	C
J	J	E	D	E	D	I	A	H	D	E	X	R	E	U	C	S
O	O	S	O	F	K	J	B	V	C	F	T	P	J	G	O	V
A	B	R	M	D	L	N	C	N	I	O	C	D	E	E	N	A
W	E	A	H	J	O	S	A	L	J	E	D	H	A	N	I	M
L	Q	N	E	I	C	R	L	A	L	R	I	I	N	E	C	E
A	D	H	S	A	T	E	E	R	D	M	C	A	L	R	A	L
E	R	I	N	R	A	A	E	R	G	L	I	D	S	A	T	I
W	O	L	P	B	V	D	E	Y	O	W	D	E	R	L	O	A
A	P	S	L	A	I	N	D	D	D	O	A	X	I	C	S	E
J	I	E	S	A	U	R	E	A	W	H	S	T	I	U	T	A
A	E	Q	T	H	S	Y	U	L	L	K	O	E	B	S	J	R
C	Z	C	B	N	L	J	H	E	F	D	A	R	V	T	Y	H
A	Q	W	R	Y	U	O	E	Y	T	I	L	J	G	E	D	A
S	S	X	C	V	B	N	M	U	H	Y	T	F	R	R	L	R
A	B	R	A	H	A	M	L	I	N	C	O	L	N	X	D	T

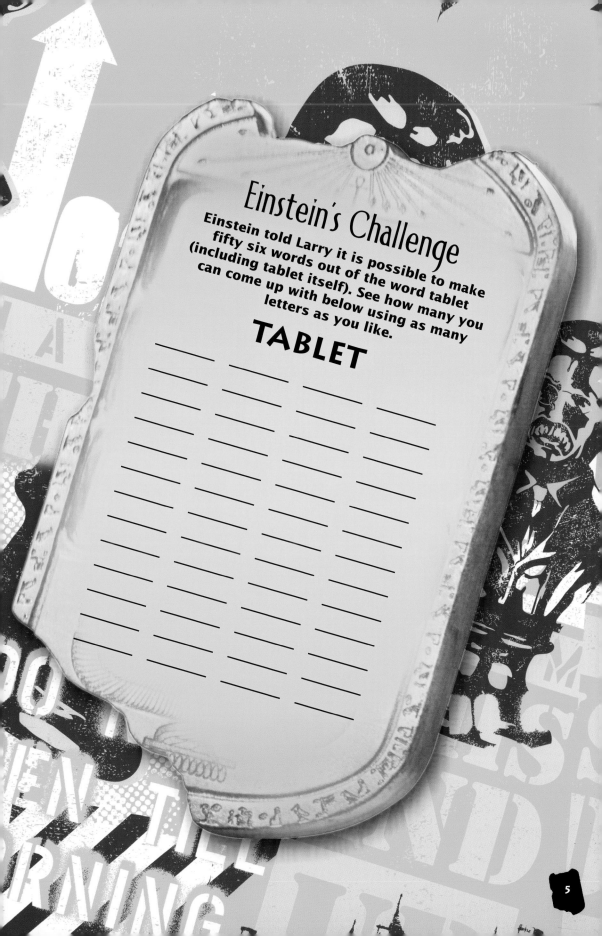

Einstein's Challenge

Einstein told Larry it is possible to make fifty six words out of the word tablet (including tablet itself). See how many you can come up with below using as many letters as you like.

TABLET

_____ _____ _____
_____ _____ _____
_____ _____ _____
_____ _____ _____
_____ _____ _____
_____ _____ _____
_____ _____ _____
_____ _____ _____
_____ _____ _____
_____ _____ _____
_____ _____ _____
_____ _____ _____
_____ _____ _____
_____ _____ _____
_____ _____ _____

Spot the Difference

Look closely at these two pictures of the Cherubs. Can you find six differences between them?

Monkeying Around

**Only one of these is the real Able.
Which one is it?**

A

B

C

D

Too Many Torches

Larry Daley invented a glow in the dark torch. How many of them can you count here?

Key to Life

When the sun sets, everything in the museum comes to life! Crack the code to work out which of the exhibits holds the magic.

— NIGHT & MUSEUM 2 —

A _____   L _____

B _____   M _____

E _____   N _____

F _____   O _____

H _____   R _____

K _____   T _____

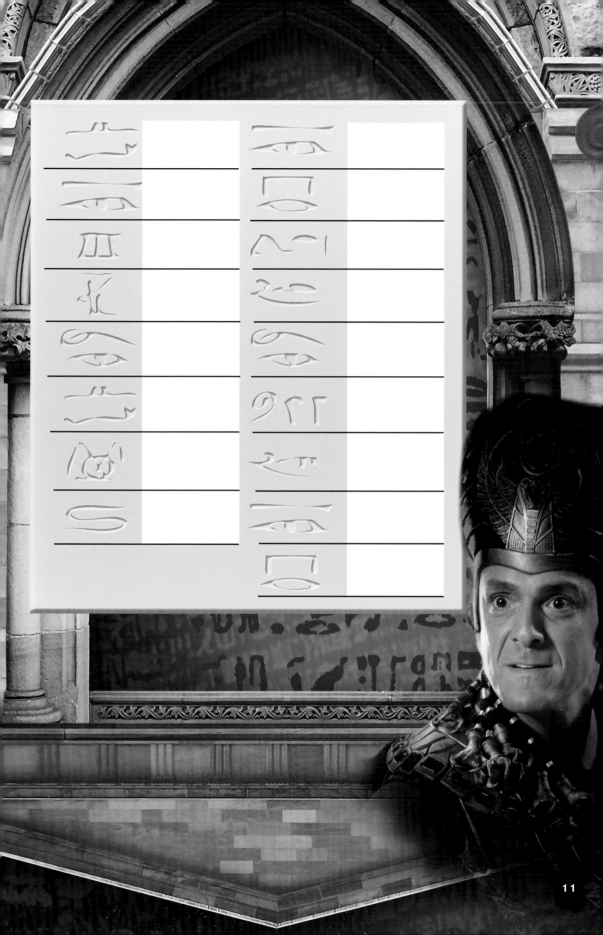

Cherub Tic-Tac-Toe

Find a friend to play this game with. One of you will be bows and one will be arrows. Take turns drawing your symbol in the grid. The aim of the game is to get three of your symbols in a row.

Memory Game

Examine the picture below then turn the page and see how many questions about it you can answer.

What Can You Remember?

1. What colour is the giant cube?

2. How many trees are there in the picture?

3. Is the floor tiled or carpeted?

4. Which character is in the picture?

5. What colour is the character's hat?

Odd Ivan Out

**One of these pictures of Ivan the Terrible
is different to the others, but which is it?**

Quick Quiz

How much do you remember from
the film *Night at the Museum 2:*
Test your memory with this quick quiz!

1. WHAT KIND OF DINOSAUR
   DOES LARRY PLAY WITH IN
   THE NEW YORK NATURAL
   HISTORY MUSEUM?
   A. Diplodocus
   B. Tyrannosaurus Rex
   C. Pterodactyl

2. AMELIA EARHART WAS
   THE FIRST FEMALE WHAT?
   A. Pilot
   B. Plumber
   C. Astronaut

3. WHAT ARE DEXTER AND
   ABLE?
A. Egyptians
B. Statues
C. Monkeys

4. WHO DOES KAHMUNRAH
   PUT IN AN HOURGLASS?
A. Jed
B. Larry
C. Octavius

5. WHERE DO LARRY AND
   AMELIA MEET ABRAHAM
   LINCOLN?
A. The Air and Space Museum
B. The Lincoln Memorial
C. The White House

6. WHAT IS SPECIAL
   ABOUT THE TORCH
   LARRY DESIGNS?
A. It glows in the dark
B. It is indestructible
C. It works underwater

The Great Gallery Grab

Find a friend to play this game with and see how many museum artefacts you can collect. Take turns joining up any two dots. Whenever you make a complete square, write your initials in it. Score one point for each square and five points for a square with an artefact in it.

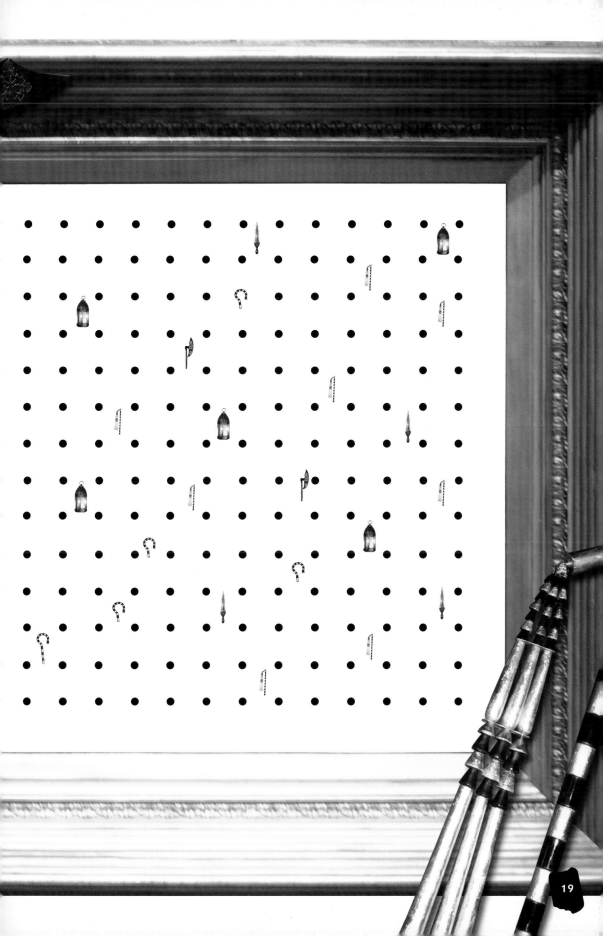

Squid Sketch

Copy each square of the picture into the bigger grid to draw your own giant squid.

Catch the Monkey

Able has stolen the tablet. Find your way through the maze to get it back from him before it gets into the wrong hands!

START

EXIT

The Bigger Picture

Which of the smaller pictures below can you find in the bigger picture? Circle the ones you can see.

Art Gallery

The Tablet of Ahkmenrah brings paintings and photographs to life as well as the exhibits. Draw or paint your own pictures to create your own art gallery and see if the Tablet brings them to life!

Alphabet Code

Crack the code on the Tablet of Ahkmenrah by writing the previous letter of the alphabet in each case to reveal its riddle.

A B C D E F G
H I J K L M N
O P Q R S T
U V W X Y Z

ZPV / XJMM / GJOE / UIF /

DPNCJOBUJPO / ZPV /

TFFL, / JG /

ZPV / GJHVSF / PVU /

UIF / TFDSFU / BU / UIF /

IFBSU / PG /

UIF / UPNC.

Bad Guys Wordsearch

See if you can find all the bad guys from the museums in this wordsearch. They can be hidden horizontally, vertically, diagonally and even backwards!

Al Capone
Attila the Hun
Egyptians

Gangsters
Ivan the Terrible
Kahmunrah

Napoleon Bonaparte
Streltsi soldiers

W	Q	E	G	Y	P	T	I	A	N	S	D	F	G	H	J	E
X	C	V	B	N	H	G	F	D	S	A	Q	R	T	E	T	I
S	T	R	E	L	T	S	I	S	O	L	D	I	E	R	S	V
A	S	Q	S	E	R	G	H	T	R	E	C	V	A	B	N	A
X	O	R	U	V	B	C	F	R	D	S	A	P	L	R	D	N
S	W	E	E	B	K	A	H	M	H	R	A	P	C	O	O	T
A	T	I	L	T	N	H	E	D	S	N	W	S	A	P	H	H
V	C	D	E	W	S	Z	S	A	O	D	E	F	P	T	R	E
Q	A	E	D	F	R	G	C	B	X	S	E	G	O	B	Y	T
N	B	G	T	R	E	S	N	C	F	T	T	Y	N	D	S	E
M	N	H	Y	T	R	O	E	A	S	D	R	G	E	E	V	R
B	T	Y	H	J	E	L	Y	P	G	I	J	K	Y	T	R	R
A	T	T	I	L	A	T	H	E	H	U	N	H	G	F	D	I
W	E	D	O	A	S	E	D	F	T	H	Y	E	W	C	V	B
B	Y	P	T	R	K	A	H	M	U	N	R	A	H	V	F	L
W	A	Z	X	C	V	B	N	M	L	K	J	H	G	F	D	E
N	D	S	A	Q	W	E	T	R	Y	U	I	O	P	L	I	G

Hide and Seek

Able and the three cherubs are playing hide and seek in the art museum. Can you find them in this picture?

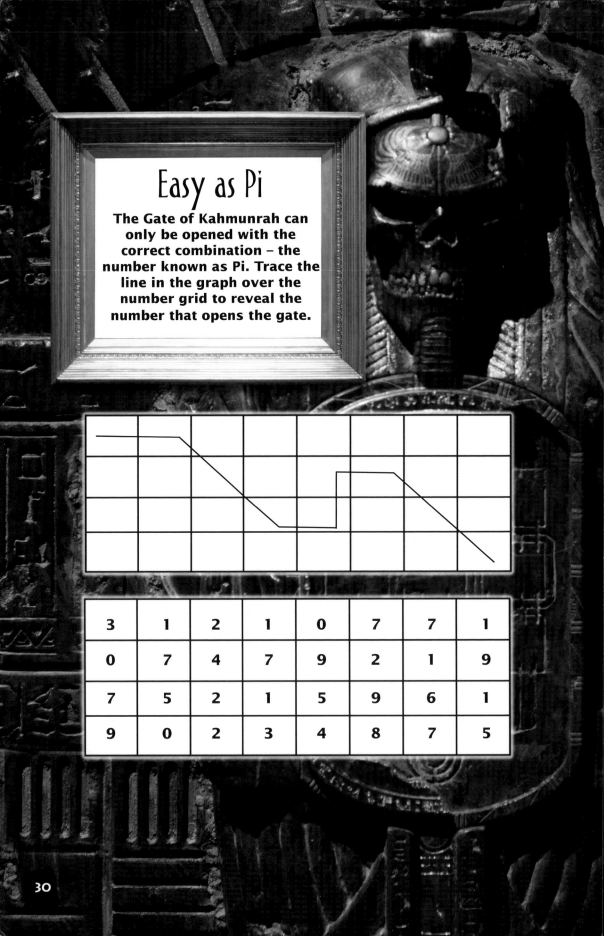

Easy as Pi

The Gate of Kahmunrah can only be opened with the correct combination – the number known as Pi. Trace the line in the graph over the number grid to reveal the number that opens the gate.

3	1	2	1	0	7	7	1
0	7	4	7	9	2	1	9
7	5	2	1	5	9	6	1
9	0	2	3	4	8	7	5

Answers

PAGE 2 Escape!

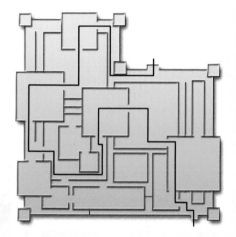

PAGE 4
Good Guys Wordsearch

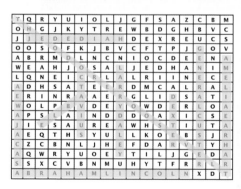

PAGE 6 Spot the Difference

PAGE 8 Monkeying Around
C is the real Able.

PAGE 9 Too Many Torches
There are 24 torches.

PAGE 10 Key to Life

The Tablet of Ahkmenrah
brings everything to life.

PAGE 14 What Can You Remember?
1. Red.
2. Four.
3. Tiled.
4. Napoleon Bonaparte
5. black.

PAGE 15 Odd Ivan Out
A is the odd one out.

PAGE 16 Quick Quiz
1. B, 2. A, 3. C, 4. A, 5. B, 6. A.

PAGE 21 Catch the Monkey

PAGE 22 The Bigger Picture

PAGE 26 Alphabet Code
The code says "You will find the combination you seek, if you figure out the secret at the heart of the tomb."

PAGE 28 Bad Guys Wordsearch

W	Q	E	G	Y	P	T	I	A	N	S	D	F	G	H	J	E
X	C	V	B	N	H	G	F	D	S	A	Q	R	T	E	T	I
S	T	R	E	L	T	S	I	S	O	L	D	I	E	R	S	V
A	S	Q	S	E	R	G	H	T	R	E	C	V	A	B	N	A
X	O	R	U	V	B	C	F	R	D	S	A	P	L	R	D	N
S	W	E	E	B	K	A	H	M	H	R	A	P	C	O	O	T
A	T	I	L	T	N	H	E	D	S	N	W	S	A	P	H	H
V	C	D	E	W	S	Z	S	A	O	D	E	F	P	T	R	E
Q	A	E	D	F	R	G	C	B	X	S	E	G	O	B	Y	T
N	B	G	T	R	E	S	N	C	F	T	T	Y	N	D	S	E
M	N	H	Y	T	R	O	E	A	S	D	R	G	E	E	V	R
B	T	Y	H	J	E	L	Y	P	G	I	J	K	Y	T	R	I
A	T	T	I	L	A	T	H	E	H	U	N	H	G	F	D	I
W	E	D	O	A	S	E	D	F	T	H	Y	E	W	C	V	B
B	Y	P	T	R	K	A	H	M	U	N	R	A	H	V	F	L
W	A	Z	X	C	V	B	N	M	L	K	J	H	G	F	D	E
N	D	S	A	Q	W	E	T	R	Y	U	I	O	P	L	I	G

PAGE 29 Hide and Seek

PAGE 30 Easy as Pi.
The number is 3.14159265